NEW DAD JOKES

A DAD JOKE A DAY TO HELP YOU GET THROUGH THE FIRST SLEEPLESS YEAR

By William Harding

Just For you!

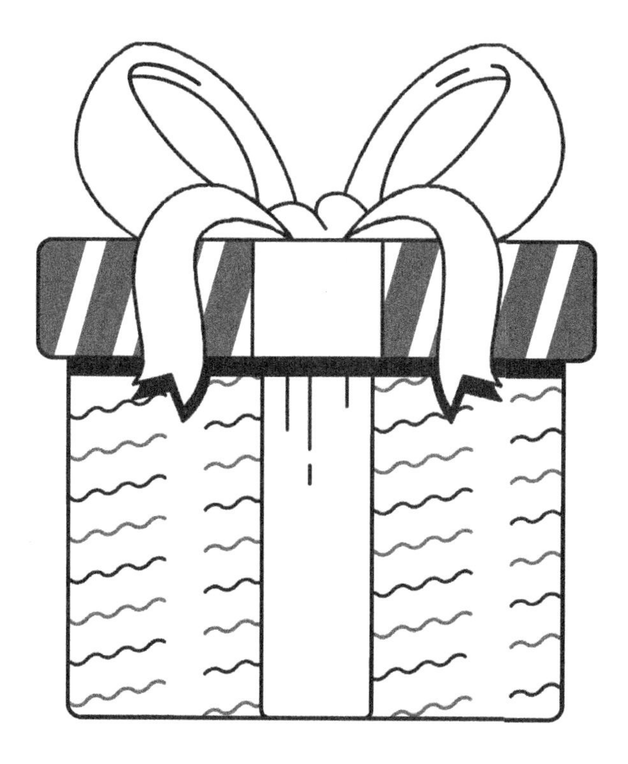

A FREE GIFT TO OUR READERS

10 Step **Action** plan that you can download now. Feel confident and prepared for your new born right now

CONGRATULATION, DAD!

Welcome to the world of fatherhood! Congratulations on becoming a first-time dad. Your life is about to change in ways you never imagined, filled with sleepless nights, diaper changes, and an endless supply of baby wipes. But fear not, because along with the challenges come moments of pure joy and laughter.

As a new dad, you're embarking on a journey filled with unforgettable experiences, from baby's first steps to hearing their first words (which might just be "Dada" if you're lucky). It's a rollercoaster ride of emotions, and a great sense of humor will be your trusty sidekick.

In this joke book, we've compiled a collection of lighthearted and relatable jokes specifically tailored for first-time dads like you. Whether you need a good laugh after a long night of soothing a fussy baby or you want to share a chuckle with fellow dads in the trenches, these jokes are here to brighten your day.

So, kick back, take a break from changing diapers, and enjoy these dad-approved jokes. Because being a dad is a wild adventure, and laughter is the best way to navigate the twists and turns. Get ready to embrace the world of parenting with open arms and a hearty laugh!

Remember, you're not alone on this journey. Let the humor in these pages remind you that you're part of a community of dads who have been there, done that, and survived to tell the tale. Happy parenting and happy laughing!

Feel free to modify this introduction as needed to fit the tone and style of your joke book!

DAY 1

Q: Why did the dad always take a pencil to bed?

A: He liked to draw his “dreams”!

…………………………..

DAY 2

Q: Why did the dad tomato turn red?

A: Because he saw the salad dressing!

………………………

DAY 3

Q: Why did the parent computer sit down with their child computer?

A: Because they wanted to have a byte together!

…………………………..

DAY 4

Q: I told my wife she was drawing her eyebrows too high

A: She looked surprised!

…………………………..

DAY 5

Q: Where does the dad pig leave his car?

A: The porking lot

…………………………..

DAY 6

Q: Why did the dad take up gardening?

A: Because he wanted to "grow" as a person!

…………………………..

DAY 7

Q: How do you organize a space party for new dads?

A: You "planet" and make sure there are plenty of dad jokes!

……………………….

DAY 8

Q: Did you hear about the dad who won the baking contest?

A: He had a "batter" idea than the rest!

……………………….

DAY 9

Q: Why don't new dads ever get lost?

A: Because they always have their "dad-compass" with them!

……………………….

DAY 10

Q: How do new dads stay cool in the summer?

A: They use their "dad-vantage" and wear socks with sandals!

…………………………

DAY 11

Q: Did you hear about the new dad who opened a bakery?

A: He wanted to make some "dad-pancakes"!

…………………………

QUICK HACK

Get yourself a daddy notebook. In it, leave a page or two at the beginning to brainstorm ideas about what you need to include in your budgeting or just to doodle. Don't think of it as a chore, and make it your own. The more fun you have with it, the more you will use it. The importance of writing out a budget and seeing how to meet it realistically cannot be understated.

DAY 12

Q: Why did the new dad bring a ladder to the store?

A: Because he heard the prices were "sky-high"!

....

DAY 13

Q: Why was the new dad always reading parenting books?

A: He wanted to be a "father-knower"!

....

DAY 14

Q: How did the new dad handle the baby's crying?

A: He rocked it like a "dad-io station"!

....

DAY 15

Q: Why did the first-time dad bring a ladder to the baby's room?

A: Because he heard the baby was a little "climber"!

…………………………..

DAY 16

Q: What's a first-time dad's favorite type of music?

A: Heavy "nappy"!

…………………………..

DAY 17

Q: Why did the first-time dad call the baby's crib "the office"?

A: Because that's where the "diaper changes" happen!

…………………………..

DAY 18

Q: Why did the first-time dad take a nap in the baby's crib?

A: Because he wanted to be "in-cradle-able"!

…………………………..

DAY 19

Q: How does a first-time dad calm a fussy baby?

A: He tells them, "Don't worry, we're in this 'crib' together!"

…………………………..

DAY 20

Q: Why did the first-time dad bring a ladder to the playground?

A: He wanted to see things from a "slide" perspective!

…………………………..

DAY 21

Q: What's the difference between a baby and a baked potato?

A: About 140 calories

…………………………..

DAY 22

Q: Why did the mom demand a paycheck from the hospital?

A: To compensate her for her labor!

…………………………..

DAY 23

Q: What do you call a fish with no eyes?

A: Fsh.

…………………………..

DAY 24

I'm reading a book on anti-gravity. It's impossible to put down!

…………………………..

DAY 25

Q: What did the janitor say when he jumped out of the closet?

A: Supplies!

…………………………..

DAY 26

Q: How do you know when you're a parent?

A: When you start using baby wipes for everything!

…………………………..

DAY 27

Q: How do you know when you're a parent?

A: When you find yourself saying, "Because I said so!" and "Don't make me come up there!"

....

DAY 28

Parenting tip: If your child refuses to nap, just tell them it's a "silent disco" in their room.

....

DAY 29

Parenthood is discovering that "me time" now means getting to use the bathroom alone.

....

DAY 30

Q: Why was the math book sad?

A: Because it had too many problems.

…………………………..

DAY 31

Q: How do you make a tissue dance? You put a little boogie in it

A: You put a little boogie in it

…………………………..

DAY 32

Q: Why don't some couples go to the gym?

A: Because some relationships don't work out!

…………………………..

DAY 33

Q: Relationships are a lot like algebra.

A: You look at your X and wonder Y.

....

DAY 34

Q: Did you hear about the bored banker?

A: They lost interest in everything!

....

DAY 35

Q: To the person who invented Zero

A: Thanks for nothing

....

DAY 36

Q: How many apples grow on a tree

A: All of them

…………………………..

DAY 37

Q: Can a kangaroo jump higher than a house?

A: Of course, Houses cant jump!

…………………………..

DAY 38

Q: What do you call a baby that turns into a frog?

A: A toddler

…………………………..

DAY 39

Q: What's the difference between ignorance and indifference?

A: I don't know, and I don't care.

…………………………..

DAY 40

Q: Did you hear about the mathematician who's afraid of negative numbers?

A: He'll stop at nothing to avoid them.

…………………………..

DAY 41

Q: Hear about the new restaurant called Karma?

A: There's no menu: You get what you deserve.

…………………………..

DAY 42

Q: A man tells his doctor, "Doc, help me. I'm addicted to Twitter!"

A: The doctor replies, "Sorry, I don't follow you …"

…………………………..

DAY 43

Q: What do you call a fake noodle?

A: An impasta.

…………………………..

DAY 44

Q: What's a first-time dad's favorite way to relax after a busy day?

A: Dad-itation" – quiet time with baby cuddles!

…………………………..

DAY 45

Q: Why did the frog take the bus to work today?

A: His car got toad away.

…………………………..

QUICK HACK

Now is your time to start building rituals. Some of these might only last through pregnancy, but all can be helpful, and some can improve the quality of life for your whole family for the long haul. You want to focus on being the hall monitor for anything that your partner does that she may forget could cause risk to the baby. You need to be gentle and empathetic about your approach. That doesn't mean setting up spy cams or flying drones around to follow every step she takes — unless it is a joke, and you know you won't scare her to death.

…………………………..

DAY 46

Q: Why don't skeletons fight each other?

A: They don't have the guts.

…………………………..

DAY 47

Q: How do you organize a space party?

A: You "planet"!

…………………………..

DAY 48

Relationships are like a deck of cards. You start with two hearts and a diamond, and you end up looking for a club and a spade.

…………………………..

DAY 49

Q: Want to hear a joke about a piece of paper?

A: Never mind…its tearable.

…………………………..

DAY 50

Q: Where do surfers learn to surf?

A: At boarding school.

…………………………..

DAY 51

Q: Why didn't the invisible man go to the dance?

A: He didn't have any body to take.

…………………………..

DAY 52

Q: "'Dad, did you get a haircut?'.

A: 'No, I got them all cut!'"

…………………………..

DAY 53

Q: What would happen if you threw all the books in the ocean?

A: It would cause a title wave.

…………………………..

DAY 54

Q: What's the best kind of bird to work for at a construction company?

A: A crane.

…………………………..

DAY 55

Q: "I got fired from my job as a taxi driver.

A: It turns out nobody thought I was fare."

…………………………..

DAY 56

Q: Where do fish keep their money?

A: In a river bank.

…………………………..

DAY 57

Q: Who stole my depression medication ?

A: I hope you're happy now.

…………………………..

DAY 58

Q: Why do bees have sticky hair?

A: Because they use a honeycomb.

…………………………..

DAY 59

Q: What happens when a snowman throws a tantrum?

A: He has a meltdown.

…………………………..

DAY 60

Q: My extra winter weight is finally gone.

A: Now, I have spring rolls.

…………………………..

DAY 61

Q: When does a joke become a dad joke?

A: When it becomes apparent.

…………………………..

DAY 62

When I was a kid, my dad got fired from his job as a road worker for theft. I refused to believe he could do such a thing, but when I got home, the signs were all there.

…………………………..

DAY 63

Q: What did one plate say to another plate?

A: Tonight, dinner's on me.

…………………………..

DAY 64

Q: What's the least-spoken language in the world?

A: Sign language.

…………………………..

DAY 65

Q: What's the best way to watch a fly-fishing tournament?

A: Live stream.

…………………………..

DAY 66

Q: Why did the man name his dogs Rolex and Timex?

A: Because they were watchdogs.

…………………………..

DAY 67

Q: What do you call a dog that can do magic?

A: A Labracabrador

…………………………..

DAY 68

Q: What is the Easter bunny's favorite type of music?

A: Hip-hop.

…………………………..

DAY 69

Q: How does the man in the moon get his hair cut?

A: Eclipse it.

…………………………..

DAY 70

Q: Did you hear about the restaurant on the moon?

A: Great food, no atmosphere.

…………………………..

DAY 71

Q: Did you hear the one about the kid who started a business tying shoelaces on the playground?

A: It was a knot-for-profit.

…………………………..

DAY 72

Q: Did you hear the rumor about butter?

A: Well, I'm not going to spread it!

…………………………..

DAY 73

Q: Why do melons have weddings?

A: Because they cantaloupe

…………………………..

DAY 74

Q: Why was the pig covered in ink?

A: Because it lived in a pen.

…………………………..

DAY 75

Q: Did you hear about the guy who stole 50 cartons of hand sanitizer?

A: They couldn't prosecute—his hands were clean.

…………………………..

DAY 76

Q: What do you call a snitching scientist?

A: A lab rat.

…………………………..

DAY 77

Q: Why do nurses like red crayons?

A: Sometimes they have to draw blood

…………………………..

DAY 78

Q: What do you call someone with no body and no nose?

A: Nobody knows.

…………………………..

DAY 79

My dentist offered me dentures for only a dollar. It sounded like a good deal at the time, but now I have buck teeth.

…………………………..

DAY 80

Q: What did one wall say to the other wall?

A: "I'll meet you at the corner!"

…………………………..

DAY 81

Q: Why did the bicycle fall over?

A: Because it was two-tired!

…………………………..

DAY 82

Q: Did you hear about the cheese factory that exploded?

A: There was nothing left but de-brie!

…………………………..

DAY 83

Q: Why did the tomato turn red?

A: Because it saw the salad dressing!

…………………………..

DAY 84

Q: How do you catch a squirrel?

A: Climb a tree and act like a nut!

…………………………..

DAY 85

Q: Why did the egg hide?

A: It was a little chicken.

…………………………..

DAY 86

Q: What did the dirt say to the rain?

A: If you keep this up, my name will be mud!

…………………………..

DAY 87

Q: Why couldn't the sunflower ride its bike?

A: It lost its petals

…………………………..

DAY 88

Q: What's an egg's favorite vacation spot?

A: New Yolk City.

…………………………..

DAY 89

Q: What kind of candy do astronauts like?

A: Mars bars.

…………………………

DAY 90

Q: I used to run a dating service for chickens, but I was struggling to make hens meet.

…………………………

QUICK HACKS

Homework for the dads to be right now includes taking inventory. If you made an effort with your notebook, birthing plan, and finances, you are going to be in good shape from the planning perspective. Continue your personal growth with diet, exercise, and stress training.

DAY 91

Q: Which is faster, hot or cold?

A: Hot, because you can catch cold.

…………………………..

DAY 92

Q: My wife told me to stop acting like a flamingo, so I had to put my foot down.

…………………………..

DAY 93

Q: What did the left eye say to the right eye?

A: Between you and me, something smells.

…………………………..

DAY 94

Q: How do celebrities stay cool?

A: They have many fans.

…………………………..

DAY 95

Q: How did the student feel when he learned about electricity?

A: Totally shocked

…………………………..

DAY 96

A horse walks into a bar. The bartender says, "Why the long face?"

…………………………..

DAY 97

Q: Why did the student eat his homework?

A: Because his teacher told him it was a piece of cake.

…………………………..

DAY 98

I used to hate facial hair...but then it grew on me.

…………………………..

DAY 99

Q: Why was the coach yelling at the vending machine?

A: He wanted his quarter back.

…………………………..

DAY 100

My girlfriend left a note on the fridge that said, "This isn't working. Goodbye." I'm not sure what she's talking about. The fridge is working fine!

…………………………

DAY 101

Q: What do snowmen do in their spare time?

A: They chill

…………………………

DAY 102

Q: What do you call an elephant that doesn't matter?

A: An irrelephant.

…………………………

DAY 103

Q: What kind of music do the mummies listen to?

A: Wrap music.

…………………………..

DAY 104

Q: What happens if a seagull flies over the bay?

A: It will become a bagel (Bay-gull)!

…………………………..

DAY 105

Q: What lights up a stadium?

A: A match.

…………………………..

DAY 106

Q: How do you think the barber won the race?

A: He took a shortcut.

…………………………..

DAY 107

Q: Two monkeys share an Amazon account. What do you call them?

A: Prime mates!

…………………………..

DAY 108

Q: Why do they not play poker in the jungle?

A: There are too many cheetahs.

…………………………..

DAY 109

Q: What is the easiest way to burn 1000 calories?

A: Leave the pizza in the oven.

…………………………..

DAY 110

I used to be addicted to soap, but I'm clean now.

…………………………..

DAY 111

Q: Why did the dog cross the road?

A: To get to the barking lot!

…………………………..

DAY 112

A nurse told me, “Sorry for the wait!” I replied, “It’s alright, I’m patient.”

…………………………..

DAY 113

Q: What did one ocean say to the other ocean?

A: Nothing, they just waved.

…………………………..

DAY 114

Q: Did you hear about the actor who fell through the floorboards?

A: He was just going through a stage.

…………………………..

DAY 115

Q: What do you call an alligator in a vest?

A: An investigator

…………………………..

DAY 116

Q: What does a house wear?

A: Address!

…………………………..

DAY 117

Q: What is a dinosaur with an extensive vocabulary called?

A: Thesaurus.

…………………………..

DAY 118

Q: Who should you never trust a person writing on graph paper?

A: He is plotting something.

…………………………..

DAY 119

Q: Why was the fraction worried about marrying the decimal?

A: Because it had to convert.

…………………………..

DAY 120

Q: What did the traffic light say to the truck?

A: Don't look! I'm changing!

…………………………..

DAY 121

Q: What do snakes like to study in school?

A: Hissss-tory!

…………………………..

DAY 122

Q: What kind of music do balloons hate? Pop music.

A: Pop music.

…………………………..

DAY 123

Q: What do you call a sad strawberry?

A: A blueberry!

…………………………..

DAY 124

Q: Why can't the music teacher start his car?

A: He left his keys on his piano!

…………………………

DAY 125

Q: Did you hear about the raisin that went out with the prune?

A: Couldn't find a date

…………………………

DAY 126

Q: Who held the baby octopus ransom?

A: Squidnappers

…………………………

DAY 127

Q: What did the baby dolphin do when he didn't get his way?

A: He whaled

…………………………..

DAY 128

The other day I started a conversation with a dolphin . We just clicked

…………………………..

DAY 129

Q: What is a speech therapists favorite brand of shoes?

A: Converse

…………………………..

DAY 130

The best nap time of the day is 6.30, hands down

…………………………..

DAY 131

A banker kept pestering me with all kinds of offers, Finally I told him to leave me a loan

…………………………..

DAY 132

Q: What is the benefit of being a test tube baby?

A: Having a womb with a view

…………………………..

DAY 133

Q: Did you hear about the sandwich that couldn't stop telling jokes?

A: It was on a roll

…………………………

DAY 134

If towels could tell jokes, they'd have a very dry sense of humor.

…………………………

DAY 135

Q: Where can you find the most superheroes in one place?

A: Cape town

…………………………

DAY 136

Q: Why did the stadium get so hot after the game?

A: All of the fans left!

…………………………

DAY 137

Q: What did the two pieces of bread say on their wedding day?

A: It was loaf at first sight

…………………………

DAY 138

Q: What do you call a Frenchman wearing sandals?

A: Philippe Flop

…………………………

DAY 139

Q: What is a trombones range?

A: About 20 yards, if you've got a good arm.

…………………………

DAY 140

Q: Why don't crabs give charity?

A: They're real shellfish breed

…………………………

DAY 141

Q: Have you ever tried to eat a clock?

A: Its very time consuming.

…………………………

QUICK HACK

Professionals who use planners never write things down one time and never look at them again. Update your plans from time to time to incorporate what you learned or remembered you forgot. This means looking at your birthing plan and notebook to update everything that needs it. Change all plans that have evolved as they are bound to over time and as you gain experience.

…………………………..

DAY 142

My friend thinks he is smart. He told me an onion is the only food that makes you cry, so I threw a coconut at his face.

…………………………..

DAY 143

Q: What happens to a frog's car when it breaks down?

A: It gets toad away.

…………………………..

DAY 144

A boy asks his father, "Dad, are bugs good to eat?" "That's disgusting. Don't talk about things like that over dinner," the dad replies. After dinner the father asks, "Now, son, what did you want to ask me?" "Oh, nothing," the boy says. "There was a bug in your soup, but now it's gone."

…………………………..

DAY 145

Q: Why did the witches' team lose the baseball game?

A: Their bats flew away.

…………………………..

DAY 146

Q: Can a kangaroo jump higher than the Empire State Building?

A: Of course. The Empire State Building can't jump.

…………………………..

DAY 147

Q: Why couldn't the leopard play hide and seek?

A: Because he was always spotted.

…………………………..

DAY 148

Q: Why was six scared of seven?

A: Because seven "ate" nine.

…………………………..

DAY 149

Q: Can February march?

A: No, but April may.

…………………………..

DAY 150

Q: Teacher: "Which book has helped you the most in your life?"

A: Student: "My father's check book!"

…………………………..

DAY 151

I was wondering why the ball kept getting bigger and bigger, and then it hit me.

…………………………..

DAY 152

Q: Why does Humpty Dumpty love autumn?

A: Because Humpty Dumpty had a great fall.

…………………………..

DAY 153

Q: What do you call a pig that does karate?

A: A pork chop.

…………………………..

DAY 154

A man got hit in the head with a can of Coke, but he was alright because it was a soft drink.

…………………………..

DAY 155

Q: Why did the fish blush?

A: Because it saw the ocean's bottom.

…………………………..

DAY 156

Q: What is the tallest building in the entire world?

A: The library, because it has so many stories.

....

DAY 157

If you ever get cold, just stand in the corner of a room for a while. They're normally around 90 degrees.

....

DAY 158

Whoever invented knock knock jokes should get a no bell prize.

....

DAY 159

Q: What did the green grape say to the purple grape?

A: "Breathe, stupid!"

…………………………..

DAY 160

I went down the street to a 24-hour grocery store. When I got there, the guy was locking the front door. I said, "Hey! The sign says you're open 24 hours." He Said, "Yes, but not in a row!"

…………………………..

DAY 161

The energizer bunny was arrested on a charge of battery.

…………………………..

DAY 162

Q: Why is England the wettest country?

A: Because so many kings and queens have been reigning there.

…………………………..

DAY 163

Teacher: "What is the chemical formula for water?" Student: "HIJKLMNO." Teacher: "What are you talking about?" Student: "Yesterday you said it's H to O!"

…………………………..

DAY 164

Q: How many politicians does it take to change a light bulb?

A: Two: one to change it and another one to change it back again.

…………………………..

DAY 165

If the right side of the brain controls the left side of the body, then lefties are the only ones in their right mind.

…………………………..

DAY 166

Q: What do you get when you cross a fish and an elephant?

A: Swimming trunks.

…………………………..

DAY 167

Q: What do clouds do when they become rich?

A: They make it rain!

…………………………..

DAY 168

Q: What did the big chimney say to the little chimney?

A: "You're too young to smoke."

....

DAY 169

Q: What is the difference between a teacher and a train?

A: One says, "Spit out your gum," and the other says, "Choo choo choo!"

....

DAY 170

Q: How do trees access the internet?

A: They log in.

....

DAY 171

Q: What happens once in a minute and twice in a moment but never in a decade?

A: The letter "m."

…………………………

DAY 172

Q: Did your hear about the man with a broken left arm and broken left leg?

A: Don't worry he's "ALRIGHT" now!

…………………………

DAY 173

Q: What is the color of the wind?

A: Blew.

…………………………

DAY 174

Q: Why shouldn't you write with a broken pencil?

A: Because it’s pointless!

…………………………..

DAY 175

Q: Why is Peter Pan always flying?

A: Because he neverlands.

…………………………..

DAY 176

Q: What do you call someone without a nose or a body?

A: Nobodynose.

…………………………..

DAY 177

Q: Why are ghosts such good cheerleaders?

A: Because they have a lot of spirit!

…………………………..

DAY 178

A lot of people cry when they cut an onion. The trick is not to form an emotional bond.

…………………………..

DAY 179

Son: "Dad, when will I be old enough so I don't have to ask mom for her permission to go out?" Dad: "Son, even I haven't grown old enough to go out without her permission!"

…………………………..

DAY 180

A man called his child's doctor, "Hello! My son just snatched my pen when I was writing and swallowed it. What should I do?" The doctor replied, "Until I can come over, write with another pen."

....

DAY 181

Q: Why did Captain Kirk go in to the ladies room?

A: Because he wanted to go where no man had gone before.

....

DAY 182

Q: What do you call a belt with a watch on it?

A: A waist of time.

....

DAY 183

Q: What can you give and keep at the same time?

A: A cold!

…………………………..

DAY 184

Q: What did the banana say to the doctor?

A: "I'm not peeling well."

…………………………..

DAY 185

Q: What did the judge say when a skunk walked into the courtroom?

A: "Odor in the court!"

…………………………..

NEW DAD HACKS

The home needs to be ready for the new arrival, and all your plans should be in place. If you have been working on them even a few minutes a week and doing monthly reviews, everything should be in pretty good order. Don't let that fool you. Keep up with what you know you have to do.

....

DAY 186

Q: Why do centipedes have 100 legs?

A: So they can walk.

....

DAY 187

Q: Why didn't the melons get married?

A: Because they cantaloupe.

....

DAY 188

Q: If a plane crashed on the Canada/USA border, where would the survivors be buried?

A: You don't bury survivors.

…………………………

DAY 189

Q: Why did Cinderella get kicked off the soccer team?

A: Because she ran away from the ball.

…………………………

DAY 190

Q: What did the cross-eyed teacher say?

A: I can't control my pupils!

…………………………

DAY 191

Q: Why are vampires so easy to fool?

A: Because they are suckers.

…………………………..

DAY 192

Q: Why didn't the sailors play cards?

A: Because the captain was on the deck.

…………………………..

DAY 193

Q: Why did the runner stop listing to music?

A: Because she broke too many records.

…………………………..

DAY 194

Q: How do birds fly?

A: They just wing it!

…………………………..

DAY 195

Q: What did the pop star do when he locked himself out?

A: He sang until he found the right key!

…………………………..

DAY 196

Q: What do you call a lawyer who has gone bad?

A: Senator.

…………………………..

DAY 197

Q: Wanna hear a joke about construction?

A: : Never mind, I'm still working on it.

……………………….

DAY 198

Q: What do you do with a sick boat?

A: Take it to the doc.

……………………….

DAY 199

Q: Why did the tofu cross the road?

A: To prove he wasn't chicken.

……………………….

DAY 200

Q: Did you hear about the guy who drank 8 Cokes?

A: He burped 7Up.

…………………………..

DAY 201

Q: What does a nosy pepper do?

A: It gets jalapeño business.

…………………………..

DAY 202

Q: What did the magnet say to the other magnet?

A: I find you very attractive!

…………………………..

DAY 203

Q: Why did the skeleton cross the road?

A: To get to the body shop.

…………………………..

DAY 204

Q: What did the beaver say to the tree?

A: "It's been nice gnawing you!"

…………………………..

DAY 205

Q: What has four wheels and flies?

A: garbage truck.

…………………………..

DAY 206

Q: What stays in one corner but travels around the world?

A: A stamp.

…………………………..

DAY 207

Q: What did the lawyer name his daughter?
A: Sue.

…………………………..

DAY 208

Q: What happens when you cross a shark with a cow?

A: I don't know but I wouldn't milk it.

…………………………..

DAY 209

Q: What kind of shoes do ninjas wear?

A: Sneakers.

…………………………..

DAY 210

Q: What did the math book say to its therapist?

A: I've got a lot of problems.

…………………………..

DAY 211

Q: Why did the one armed man cross the road?

A: To get to the second hand shop.

…………………………..

DAY 212

Q: Where do you learn how to make ice cream?

A: Sundae School

…………………………..

DAY 213

Q: What is a tree's favorite drink?

A: Root beer.

…………………………..

DAY 214

Son: "Dad, there is someone at the door to collect donations for a community swimming pool." Father: "Okay, give him a glass of water."

…………………………..

DAY 215

Q: Who earns a living by driving his customers away?

A: A taxi driver.

....

DAY 216

Q: Why are fish easy to weigh?

A: Because they have their own scales.

....

DAY 217

Ben: "Dad, there is a hole in my shoe." Dad: "Yes, Ben, that's where you put your foot."

....

DAY 218

Q: A cowboy left Montana to go to Texas on Friday and came back on Friday. How did he do it?

A: He named his horse Friday.

....

DAY 219

Man- What would you do if I won the lottery? Woman- Take half and leave! Man- Well, I won 20 bucks, here's 10, now get out!

....

DAY 220

Q: What do you get when you drop a piano down a mine shaft

A: "A miner be flat" (A minor B-flat).

....

DAY 221

Q: Did you hear about the fire at the shoe factory?

A: Unfortunately, many soles were lost.

…………………………..

DAY 222

Q: What kind of fish knows how to do an appendectomy?

A: A Sturgeon.

…………………………..

DAY 223

Q: How do you hire a horse?

A: Put up a ladder.

…………………………..

DAY 224

Q: My manager told me to have a good day.

A: So I didn't go into work.

…………………………..

DAY 225

Q: What do kids play when they have nothing else to do?

A: Bored games.

…………………………..

DAY 226

Q: What did the boy say to his fingers?

A: I'm counting on you.

…………………………..

DAY 227

Q: What does cake and baseball have in common?

A: They both need a batter.

…………………………..

DAY 228

Q: When does Friday come before Thursday?

A: In the dictionary.

…………………………..

DAY 229

Q: What did the tree say when spring finally arrived?

A: What a re-leaf.

…………………………..

DAY 230

Q: Did you hear about the guy who afraid of hurdles?

A: He got over it.

…………………………..

DAY 231

Q: Why did the drum go to bed?

A: It was beat.

…………………………..

DAY 232

Q: What do you call a rude cow?

A: Beef jerky.

…………………………..

DAY 233

Q: Have you ever had a bad sausage?

A: It's the wurst.

....

DAY 234

Q: Did you hear about the cat that ate a lemon?

A: Now it's a sour puss.

....

DAY 235

Q: What did one volcano say to the other?

A: I lava you.

....

DAY 236

Q: Why did the computer catch cold?

A: It left a window open.

…………………………..

DAY 237

Q: How do mice floss their teeth?

A: With string cheese.

…………………………..

DAY 238

Q: How do you cook an alligator?

A: With a croc-pot.

…………………………..

DAY 239

Q: What did the earthquake say when it was done?

A: Sorry, my fault!

…………………………

DAY 240

Q: Why did the computer go to bed?

A: It needed to crash.

…………………………

DAY 241

Q: What do you give the dentist of the year?

A: A little plaque.

…………………………

DAY 242

Q: What should you do to prevent dry skin?

A: Use a towel.

…………………………..

DAY 243

Q: How can you tell when a comic passes gas?

A: Something smells funny.

…………………………..

DAY 244

Q: What do you call a can opener that doesn't work?

A: A can't opener.

…………………………..

DAY 245

Q: Did you hear about the bossy man at the bar?

A: He ordered everyone around.

…………………………..

DAY 246

Q: I wanted to take a bath, but decided to leave it where it is.

…………………………..

DAY 247

Q: Did you hear about the woman who couldn't stop collecting magazines?

A: She had issues.

…………………………..

DAY 248

Q: What do you call a cow with two legs?

A: Lean beef.

…………………………..

DAY 249

Q: What sits on the seabed and has anxiety?

A: A nervous wreck.

…………………………..

NEW DAD HACK

Handle With Care. Just like shipping a rare vase, handling your baby should be done with the utmost care. Make sure to support your baby's head and neck every time you pick them up. If you have to bend down, make sure to bend your knees and pull the baby close to your chest.

DAY 250

Q: What do you call a man wearing a rug on his head?

A: Matt.

…………………………

DAY 251

Q: What's the best air to breathe if you want to be rich?

A: Millionaire.

…………………………

DAY 252

Q: Why did the girl toss a clock out the window?

A: She wanted to see time fly.

…………………………

DAY 253

Q: Where do armies belong?

A: In your sleeves.

…………………………..

DAY 254

Q: What did one plate say to another plate?

A: Tonight, dinner's on me.

…………………………..

DAY 255

Q: Did you hear about the king that went to the dentist?

A: He needed to get crowns.

…………………………..

DAY 256

Q: What happens when doctors get frustrated?

A: They lose their patients.

…………………………..

DAY 257

Q: What invention allows us to see through walls? Windows.

A: Windows.

…………………………..

DAY 258

Q: Why do nurses like red crayons?

A: Sometimes they have to draw blood.

…………………………..

DAY 259

Q: What do you call a cheese that isn't yours?

A: Nacho cheese!

…………………………

DAY 260

Q: Why did the cowboy adopt a wiener dog?

A: He wanted to get a long little doggie.

…………………………

DAY 261

Q: What's more unbelievable than a talking dog?

A: A spelling bee.

…………………………

DAY 262

Q: What kind of music scares balloons?

A: Pop music.

…………………………..

DAY 263

Q: What do dogs and phones have in common?

A: Both have collar ID.

…………………………..

DAY 264

Q: Why did the employee get fired from the keyboard factory?

A: He wasn’t putting in enough shifts.

…………………………..

DAY 265

Q: Did you hear about the man who cut off his left leg?

A: He's all right now.

……………………………

DAY 266

Q: Did you hear the one about the claustrophobic astronaut?

A: He just needed a little space.

……………………………

DAY 267

Q: What kind of music should you listen to while fishing?

A: Something catchy!

……………………………

DAY 268

Q: What do you call a girl in the middle of a tennis court?

A: Annette.

…………………………

DAY 269

Q: Did you hear about the cold dinner?

A: It was chili.

…………………………

DAY 270

Q: Why did the deer go to the dentist?

A: It had buck teeth.

…………………………

DAY 271

Q: Where does a sheep go to get a haircut?

A: The baa baa shop.

…………………………..

DAY 272

Q: What did the mama cow say to the baby cow?

A: It's pasture bed time.

…………………………..

DAY 273

Q: Why should you never use a dull pencil?

A: Because it's pointless.

…………………………..

DAY 274

Q: Why did the cookie go to the doctor?

A: It was feeling crumby.

…………………………

DAY 275

Q: Where did the cat go after losing its tail?

A: The retail store.

…………………………

DAY 276

Q: Why don't eggs tell jokes?

A: They'd crack each other up.

…………………………

DAY 277

Q: What do you call a herd of sheep falling down a hill?

A: lambslide.

…………………………..

DAY 278

Q: How many tickles does it take to make an octopus laugh?

A: Ten tickles.

…………………………..

DAY 279

Q: What do you call a potato wearing glasses?

A: A spec-tater.

…………………………..

DAY 280

Q: What is a calendar's favorite food?

A: Dates.

…………………………..

DAY 281

Q: Why did the watch go on vacation?

A: To unwind.

…………………………..

DAY 282

Q: Why did the computer get glasses?

A: To improve its website.

…………………………..

DAY 283

Q: What did the blanket say to the bed?

A: I've got you covered.

…………………………..

DAY 284

Q: What did the roof say to the shingle?

A: The first one's on the house.

…………………………..

DAY 285

Q: What do you call birds that stick together?

A: Velcrows

…………………………..

DAY 286

Q: Why did the duck fall on the sidewalk?

A: He tripped on a quack.

…………………………..

DAY 287

Q: How do birds learn to fly?

A: They wing it.

…………………………..

DAY 288

Q: What did one elevator say to the other elevator?

A: I think I'm coming down with something.

…………………………..

DAY 289

Q: What did the hamburger name its baby?

A: Patty.

…………………………..

DAY 290

Q: Why did the phone wear glasses?

A: Because it lost all its contacts.

…………………………..

DAY 291

Q: Why are fish so easy to weigh?

A: Because they have their own set of scales.

…………………………..

DAY 292

Q: What do you give a scientist with bad breath?

A: Experi-mints.

…………………………..

DAY 293

Q: What did Benjamin Franklin say when he discovered electricity?

A: Nothing. He was too shocked.

…………………………..

DAY 294

Q: What do you call a medieval lamp?

A: A knight light.

…………………………..

DAY 295

Q: How can you tell the difference between a dog and tree?

A: By their bark.

…………………………

DAY 296

Q: How you fix a broken pumpkin?

A: With a pumpkin patch.

…………………………

DAY 297

Q: Where do boats go when they're sick?

A: To the dock.

…………………………

DAY 298

Q: Did you hear the rumor about butter?

A: Well, I'm not going to go spreading it!

…………………………..

DAY 299

Q: Where do books hide when they're afraid?

A: Under their covers.

…………………………..

DAY 300

Q: What did the calculator say to the pencil?

A: You can count on me.

…………………………..

DAY 301

When I see lovers' name carved in a tree, I don't think its sweet. I just think its surprising how many people bring a knife on a date!

…………………………..

DAY 302

A man asks his phone: "Siri, Why am I still single?!"

Siri activates front camera!

…………………………..

DAY 303

Dentist: "You need a crown."

Patient: "Finally someone who understands me".

…………………………..

DAY 304

I was going to tell a time traveling joke, but you guys didn't like it.

…………………………..

DAY 305

Q: What month is the shortest of the year?

A: May, it only has three letters.

…………………………..

DAY 306

I through a boomerang a few years ago, I now live in constant fear.

…………………………..

DAY 307

Q: What do you call a lazy kangaroo?

A: A pouch potato.

…………………………..

DAY 308

I used to run a dating service for chickens, but I was struggling to make hens meet.

…………………………..

DAY 309

Q: Why do we tell actors to "break a leg?"

A: Because every play has a cast.

…………………………..

DAY 310

Q: Why do oranges wear sunscreen?

A: So they don't peel.

…………………………..

DAY 311

My wife accused me of being immature, I told her get out of my fort.

…………………………..

DAY 312

Q: What do you call a fake noodle?

A: An impasta.

…………………………..

DAY 313

Q: Why does Humpty Dumpty love autumn?

A: Because he had a great fall.

…………………………..

DAY 314

Q: What happens when a strawberry gets run over crossing the street?

A: Traffic jam.

…………………………..

DAY 315

Q: How does an octopus go into battle?

A: Well-armed.

…………………………..

DAY 316

Q: Where do young trees go to learn?

A: Elementree school.

…………………………..

DAY 317

Q: What do you call a bee that can't make up its mind?

A: A Maybe.

…………………………..

DAY 318

Q: What did the mayonnaise say when the refrigerator door was opened?

A: Close the door, I'm dressing.

…………………………..

DAY 319

Q: What did the full glass say to the empty glass?

A: You look drunk.

…………………………..

DAY 320

Q: Did you hear the one about the roof?

A: Never mind, it's over your head.

…………………………..

DAY 321

Q: How do you find will smith in snow?

A: Look for the "Fresh Prints."

…………………………..

DAY 322

A designer walks into a bar. The bartender says, “Sorry, we don’t serve your type in here.”

…………………………..

DAY 323

A man walks into a library and asks the librarian for books about paranoia. She whispers, "They're right behind you!"

…………………………..

DAY 324

Q: Want to hear a roof joke?

A: The first one's on the house.

…………………………..

DAY 325

Q: What should you do if you're attacked by a group of clowns?

A: Go straight for the juggler.

…………………………..

DAY 326

Q: I saw a movie about how ships are put together.

A: It was riveting.

…………………………..

DAY 327

Q: Why did the taxi driver get fired?

A: Passengers didn't like it when she went the extra mile.

…………………………..

DAY 328

I couldn't believe that the highway department called my dad a thief. But when I got home, all the signs were there.

…………………………..

DAY 329

Q: How do mountains stay warm in the winter?

A: Snowcaps.

…………………………..

DAY 330

Q: Is this pool safe for diving?

A: It deep ends.

…………………………..

DAY 331

Q: What kind of shorts do clouds wear?

A: Thunderpants.

…………………………..

DAY 332

Q: Can February March?

A: No, but April May.

…………………………..

DAY 333

Q: What's the difference between a poorly dressed man on a unicycle and a well-dressed man on a bicycle?

A: Attire.

…………………………..

DAY 334

Q: What is the best day to go to the beach?

A: Sunday, of course.

....

DAY 335

People think "icy" is the easiest word to spell. Come to think of it, I see why.

....

DAY 336

My teachers told me I'd never amount to much because I procrastinate so much. I told them, "Just you wait!"

....

DAY 337

Q: What's the easiest way to get straight As?

A: Use a ruler.

…………………………..

DAY 338

Q: Did you hear about the painter who was hospitalized?

A: The doctors say it was due to too many strokes.

…………………………..

DAY 339

Q: What washes up on very small beaches?

A: Micro-waves.

…………………………..

DAY 340

Q: How does a farmer mend his overalls?

A: With cabbage patches.

…………………………..

DAY 341

I got my husband a fridge for his birthday. His face lit up when he opened it.

…………………………..

DAY 342

Q: Why were they called the Dark Ages?

A: Because there were lots of knights.

…………………………..

DAY 343

Q: What did the big flower say to the little flower?

A: "Hi bud!"

....

DAY 344

Q: I bought the world's worst thesaurus yesterday.

A: Not only is it terrible, it's terrible.

....

DAY 345

Q: Why aren't koalas actual bears?

A: They don't have the right koalafications.

....

DAY 346

Q: A group of crows was arrested for hanging out together.

A: The charge? Attempted murder.

…………………………..

DAY 347

Q: What time does a duck wake up?

A: The quack of dawn.

…………………………..

DAY 348

Q: Have you heard the one about the skunk?

A: Never mind, it really stinks.

…………………………..

DAY 349

Q: What do you call a pile of kittens?

A: A meowntain.

…………………………..

DAY 350

Q: What do you call a parade of rabbits marching backward?

A: A receding hare line.

…………………………..

DAY 351

Q: Why was the teddy bear not hungry?

A: Because he was already stuffed.

…………………………..

DAY 352

Q: Why do spiders make such great baseball players?

A: Because they catch flies.

…………………………..

DAY 353

Q: How does a dog stop a video?

A: By hitting the paws button.

…………………………..

DAY 354

A man walks into a library and orders a hamburger. The librarian says, "This is a library." The man apologizes and whispers, "I'd like a hamburger, please."

…………………………..

DAY 355

Q: Some people eat snails.

A: They must not like fast food.

…………………………

NEW DAD HACKS

When it comes to baby proofing, you can't be too careful. While it may be a bit before your child can roam freely, you'll want to lock down every part of your home as soon as possible. Your bedroom, your bathroom, the kitchen, the living room; find every corner, chemical, and crevice that your baby could possibly get into.

…………………………

DAY 356

Q: Did you hear about the cheese factory that exploded in France?

A: There was nothing left but de-Brie.

…………………………

DAY 357

I used to be addicted to not showering. Luckily, I've been clean for five years.

…………………………..

DAY 358

A cement mixer and a prison bus crashed on the highway. Police advise citizens to look out for a group of hardened criminals.

…………………………..

DAY 359

Q: What does the world's top dentist get?

A: A little plaque.

…………………………..

DAY 360

Q: What do you get from a pampered cow?

A: Spoiled milk.

…………………………..

DAY 361

If the early bird gets the worm, I'll sleep until there's pancakes.

…………………………..

DAY 362

If two vegetarians get into an argument, is it still called beef?

…………………………..

DAY 363

At my age I'm no longer a snack, I'm a happy meal. I come with toys and kids.

…………………………..

DAY 364

I want to organize a hide-and-seek league, but good players are hard to find.

…………………………..

DAY 365

Q: Did you hear about my neighbor?

A: 50 years old, delivers babies for a living, just bought a new car. Classic midwife crisis!

…………………………..

HOWS DAD DOING.............

IM GOING TO BE A DAD!

Date I Found Out --

My Reaction

How I Revealed To My Spouse

Immediate Family Reaction

How Did We Tell Our Loved Ones

Date

Dear Baby,

"Father is the noblest title a man can be given.

It is more than a biological role.

It signifies a patriarch, a leader, an exemplar, a confidant, a teacher, a hero, a friend."

-Robert L. Backman

Printed in Great Britain
by Amazon